DEVON
Curiosities

JANE LANGTON

BOSSINEY BOOKS

First published in 1989 by
Bossiney Books
St Teath, Bodmin, Cornwall.

Typeset and Printed by
Clowes Book Printers
St Columb, Cornwall.

Bound by R Booth (Bookbinders) Ltd
Mabe Burnthouse, Cornwall

PLATE ACKNOWLEDGMENTS
Front cover photography
by Roy Westlake
Back cover photography
by Ray Bishop

Ray Bishop: pages 7, 8, 9, 13, 35, 51,
57, 84, 89, 92, 95

Felicity Young: pages 25, 31

Roy Westlake: pages 15, 33

H O Ponting: page 14

Ken Duxbury: page 20

David Golby: pages 26, 80

Joan Rendell: pages 59, 63, 64, 68

About the author
and the book

Jane Langton, who lives in Torquay, is a member of an old established Devon family whose roots go back to the seventeenth century. Jane was for several years a well-known voice and skilful interviewer in local radio, but in 1988 she moved into the field of Westcountry newspapers – and works for the 'Herald Express' at Torquay. A Capricorn subject, she is married to John Reynolds, a senior producer/presenter at BBC Radio Devon.

In February 1989 Jane Langton made her debut as a Bossiney author, contributing a chapter on 'The Magic and Mystery of Thomas Hardy' in 'Dorset Mysteries', introduced by the distinguished novelist Jean Stubbs.

Now comes 'Devon Curiosities': a fascinating illustrated tour which proves Devon has more than her share of the strange and the freakish. Jane, with her radio and newspaper background, has something of the detective in her make-up; she can sense – and scent – an unusual, an off-beat angle. On her journeys across Devon she shows us that curiosity defies neat classification. Curiosity, like beauty, is essentially in the eye of the beholder.

The diversity of this journey across 'Glorious Devon' is remarkable. Jane invites us to visit Burgh Island and Lundy. She meets 'Uncle Tom Cobley' and enjoys a drink at The Nobody Inn at Doddiscombe. In a Dartmoor valley she discovers the last house in England to be built in a single day. She follows in the footsteps of Baring-Gould and goes to Grimspound. In South Devon she recalls a curious pair of sisters who acquired fame and notoriety in fashionable Torquay. In North Devon she reflects on holidays with her grandmother at Ilfracombe, tells about the finest raspberries in Britain and takes us up the longest street of any village in England.

A harvest of fine photographs, some ancient and some modern, make this a grand visual tour. As we travel from place to place, and page to page, we do so with a mounting sense of pleasure and anticipation, for Jane Langton possesses a rare combination of adventure and curiosity. The words and pictures make us feel we too are making this exploration among 'Devon Curiosities'.

Jane Langton

Devon Curiosities

A CURIOSITY is something fascinating, something strange. In this day and age it might also be described as an oddity.

While staying more or less faithful to the concise dictionary definition, a curiosity surely depends on time, on fashion. What was curious 100 years ago as something very new, might now be curious because it is obsolete. A case in point is the railways. My great grandmother lived in Ilfracombe in North Devon. She witnessed the arrival of steam in the town, a great event for the town that previously saw its visitors arrive by boat. New housing was erected around that part of the town. But before she died – at a ripe old age of 90 something – cuts had been made and the railway station at Ilfracombe is now put to a different use.

I was born and brough up in Devon and have spent my life travelling from the south to the north visiting relatives. But, oddly enough, only by making this journey have I discovered so many fascinating and off-beat aspects of the county. How often do we hear someone speak an unusual or quaint phrase in the middle of a conversation – and do we pause to think of its origins? Do we probe further? The odds are probably against us doing that, but authorship can be a splendid spur, encouraging one to sharpen a sense of

The author on her quest for 'Devon Curiosities' pauses on the banks of the West Dart on Dartmoor – this water eventually joins the sea down at Dartmouth on the south coast.

No, not a Stone Age jacuzzi but the remains of Bronze Age civilisation high up on Dartmoor.

curiosity. Think about the ordinary things that we use in the day to day business of living. The car, in which John and I travelled on this pursuit of the unusual, may one day end up in a motor museum; while the hockey stick I used at school in Ottery St Mary would more than likely be regarded, even now, as an 'antique'.

Geographically Devon is out on a limb. For so much of its history it has been inaccessible and some would still say that there are parts which have been left out of the grand plan of motorways and railways. The two long coastlines, north and south, have contributed to the economy through fishing, trade, exploration, holidays and even piracy and smuggling. The natural resources have been utilised in

This curiously shaped tree stood outside the churchyard at Stoke for many years. It is no more – more of a mystery perhaps.

the cloth industry and in mining. We have had our glorious moments in history, but all too often Devon has been on the fringe of something that happened elsewhere.

So what is there to write about you may ask?

Quite a lot in fact.

There are more than 30 subjects touched upon in this volume, all in alphabetical order. Much more has been left out! Once I started to investigate Devon's Curiosities I found that I could probably have filled two volumes quite easily. So if a favourite tale is missing from this volume, please don't despair. I admit to making an arbitrary decision based on my personal preferences. Different things appeal

THE contrasting coastlines of Devon, depicted in four old picture postcards. Sidmouth in 1915 and Ladram Rocks near Sidmouth on the southern flank, and North Walk and Woody Bay, in the north, both near Lynton.

11

to different people and the items chosen have captured my imagination.

Some stretch back to ancient times, to man's earliest settlement here; others are much more recent, a matter of 30 years ago but all I feel count as a 'curiosity'. I have become a time traveller. Some have personal connections; a place where I have lived, where I went to school, or maybe passed by without knowing its significance. Others I have discovered for the first time on my journey as author.

You, too, will need your imagination. Think, ponder a little, when you next look out of a window at a view. The natural landscape forms strange shapes which have prompted our ancestors to impart all sorts of qualities to it. Who knows if a tale passed on was fact or fiction? Tracing my footsteps across the sometimes wild, majestic landscape of Devon you may, perhaps, paint a picture in your mind. With each section, a new piece will form on the canvas until a whole new image has been created. It may enlarge upon, or complement, a picture that is already held. It may be something quite fresh.

Devon may have been on the edge of some milestones in British history, but we can claim, quite proudly to have produced a few heroes of our own. Though curiosity is a natural part of the human make-up, maybe Devonians have more than their fair share. Perhaps it is mixed up with ambition and, possibly, it has been the driving force behind some of the great men who were born here – Sir Francis Drake and Captain R F Scott to name just two.

Perhaps you have visited some of the places mentioned in these pages, following in the footsteps of so many others, as I did, across the moors, to the coasts – or maybe you will venture forth in the future. Whatever applies to you, enjoy these *Devon Curiosities,* for they are a part of our heritage. They are an integral part of making me, a proud Devonian.

The timeless quality of Dartmoor. Judges take a close look at Devon Longwools at Widecombe Fair.

Two Devonians who personified courage with curiosity. Captain Robert Falcon Scott in the Antarctic and the statue of Sir Francis Drake on Plymouth Hoe. Two very different sons of Devon – both of whom have gone into the heroism and folklore of the county.

The Alphington Ponies

The curious often makes news.

You only have to take a glance at a local or national newspaper to see this, so I wonder what some of the local press would have made of the Misses Durnford, who back in the 1840s were one of the sights of Torquay.

They in fact hailed from Alphington just outside of Exeter, the daughters of Colonel Durnford. On arriving in Torquay, in the early years of Queen Victoria's reign, they drove a pair of ponies in front of their carriage. Lack of money – a problem that cropped up frequently in their lives – forced them to sell their transport and it was shank's pony for them thereafter. This led to their nicknames arising from the daily constitutional they took up and down Torquay.

When promenading they always walked arm in arm, always in step, never talking to anyone but each other; it was as if other people did not exist. They were so alike in appearance they were often mistaken for twins, their striking appearance being as much due to

The Misses Durnford, known as the Alphington Ponies '. . . always arm in arm, they walked with a regimental precision.'

the heavy make-up and curious dress as their distinctive mode of walking. Many years ago Sabine Baring Gould observed in *Devonshire Characters and Strange Events* '. . . they made themselves conspicuous by introducing the bloomer arrangement in the nether latitude. This as you may well suppose was regarded as a scandal; . . . but these ladies went on their way quite unruffled.'

As I mentioned, they often had financial difficulties – to put it in the parlance of the times – despite their brother, a major in the army offering to increase their allowance if they would update their dress. They refused, and continued to dress in exactly the same way whatever time of year.

They did have a considerable amount of 'cheek' when dealing with the local traders however. On one occasion they visited a Torquay shop, gave an order, but instead of paying for it, offered half of a note; the balance would be paid, they said, when they found the other half of the note! In time the tradesmen 'wised up' to the pair and would only serve them on seeing the colour of their money, complete money that is.

On moving back to Exeter, they continued to dress in the same way. At one social occasion their conspicuous dress caught the attention of Lady Rolle who challenged a young friend, Mr Palk, son of Sir Lawrence Palk to ask one of the sisters to dance. She made a bet – if he could get one sister to dance she would buy him a set of gold and diamond shirt studs. Mr Palk, not one to refuse a challenge, accepted and boldly approached the pair. He met with the same reply from both 'I never dance except my sister be also dancing!' Mr Palk, not easily put off, promptly offered to dance with both together or in succession – he won the bet and was eventually seen wearing his fancy shirt studs!

Silver Street, Appledore.

The Golden Hind halfway down the slipway at her launch from the Appledore boatyard.

Silver Street
Appledore

The charming village of Appledore stands on a peninsula along with
Westward Ho! and Northam, at the confluence of the Taw and
Torridge estuaries. It's known that a village existed there as far back
as the eleventh century, when it was called Tawmouth. The name
Appledore could derive from the Celtic 'pwl dwr' meaning a deep
pool of water, which is possible given its geographical location, or, it
may have developed from 'where apple trees grow'. Either way, the
heyday of Appledore was the Elizabethan era, expanding along with
Bideford, as the first place within the sand bar that ships could lie up.
Some of the houses date from this period and it's possible that Silver
Street, one of a number of narrow streets, was so named to reflect the
relative affluence that the community would then have enjoyed.

Because Appledore showed great loyalty to good Queen Bess
during the Armada, she rewarded them by declaring it, and Bideford,
free ports in perpetuity. Some shipbuilding can still be found there.
The present modern yard was built in 1969 and is one of the largest
covered yards in Europe, able to build a ship 300-feet long – that's as
long as a football pitch – and float it from the dock, while Hink's yard
has been responsible for the building of replicas of boats like Drake's
Golden Hind.

Berry Pomeroy Castle

Berry Pomeroy Castle was originally the site of a manor house in the early fourteenth century, built by Norman De La Pomerai. Then the castle was built. The rocky platform was a good defensive site and the castle had curtain walls, towers and a huge gatehouse, some of which still remains. Finally another mansion was built on the site, this time inside the castle's courtyard when Edward Seymour, Duke of Somerset, bought it in 1548. But he was too ambitious in his specifications and the house was never finished. Today only the ruins remain, but it is fascinating to visit the place.

Berry Pomeroy Castle is very much on the map of haunted Devon. Many visitors get the overwhelming feeling that those empty stone window frames contain real glass windows as they did years back. The faint sound of music too has been heard – and the figure of a ghostly lady in blue has been seen at the castle.

Mysterious Berry Pomeroy Castle

Blackingstone Rock

I love a good yarn. I am an incurable romantic, legends appeal to me; I can close my eyes and see horsemen riding by, heroes, heroines, the lot.

One of the best of all our legends, if indeed it is legend at all, is that of King Arthur. Folklorists say that only the Devil is mentioned more often in local legend and I can well believe it for there are sites all over Britain that claim some sort of association with this man. It is curious that while so much is told of Arthur in Cornwall, just over the border, and also in Dorset, there is very little mentioned of him here in Devon.

Blackingstone Rock just outside of Moretonhampstead is supposed to be the spot where Arthur met and fought with the Devil. It is probably just a story that has arisen from the striking natural landscape, a crag which seems thrust from a hillside with a cleft in it.

Although Arthur is probably based on a Celtic warrior who led the resistance movement against the invading English, by the Middle Ages we had adopted him as our own king. And why not? Never let it be said that we'd keep a good story down!

Blackingstone Rock near Moretonhampstead where Arthur fought the Devil.

Totnes – The Brutus Stone

A visit to Totnes will definitely mean a stroll up and down Fore Street. Therefore make sure that you pause just above Number 51 and examine the lump of granite rock that sits there, at the side of the pavement. It is the Brutus Stone, the origin of which is open to some conjecture, but one of the tales goes thus:

Many centuries ago Brutus, the grandson of Aeneas the Trojan, was expelled from Italy after killing his father in a hunting accident. He settled in Greece after defeating the Grecian King Pendrasu, married the King's daughter, but on the advice of Diana The Oracle left to seek their fortune ... 'on an island in the western sea beyond Gaul'.

Finding the island – Britain – he is supposed to have landed at Totnes, and was so entranced with the area that is now known as the gateway to the South Hams, that he named the island Britain after himself and the town Totnes. The Brutus Stone marks the exact spot of his landing. After driving away a number of local giants Brutus

Not the most impressive resting place for a stone placed in Devon by Brutus himself, but no passer-by could fail to notice the clearly marked bit of history.

made his home there and the stone was used to make important announcements, such as the accession of monarchs. Indeed, in many other towns a 'Brodestone' was used for proclamations and as a business centre.

A more likely story? That a granite boulder was left when the water of the Dart flowed at a much higher level during the Ice Age, but whether the story is true or not, this charming mint town, dating back to the tenth century and one of just four boroughs in Devon at the time of the Norman Conquest – others being Exeter, Barnstaple and Lydford – is framed with Elizabethan, Jacobean and Georgian architecture and the town still enjoys special 'Elizabethan' days when traders dress in traditional costume.

Dartmouth -
The Butterwalk

Many people would agree with me when I say that I think Dartmouth is one of the most picturesque towns in Devon, if not in England, with its narrow curving streets, a magnificent deep water harbour and woods running right to the edge of the river. Today, the boats that make use of this marvellous, natural deep-water harbour are mainly moored at the several marinas that line the river and are used by yachtsmen for their entertainment. Some come from the Brittania Royal Naval College that sits on a hill looking out towards the river's mouth. Dartmouth was originally three settlements brought together by a prosperous period during the Crusades, and ships built on the river banks went to war for Britain from the twelfth century right up until the 1939-45 war, so the boating scene hasn't always been so balmy.

But is isn't the river that concerns me here, beautiful though it is. It is the town, and specifically a series of buildings built close to the harbour called The Butterwalk which are fascinating. Built between 1628 and 1640 on reclaimed land, mostly by Mark Hawkings, The Butterwalk is one of the best examples of Devonshire domestic architecture and is, in fact, four adjoining houses. Hawkings spent nearly £2,500 on the building, no expense was spared.

The main living rooms were at first floor level and the end house nearest the harbour had the best view of all the shipping passing up and down the Dart. The upper floors were reached by spiral staircases and still retain the 'trip steps' or stairs of uneven height designed to trip thieves and thus hopefully alert the occupants.

There are leaded windows, good panelling and, most importantly, some magnificent ceilings and overmantels for which the buildings are famous. In one of the houses, number 12, there is an incredible plaster ceiling depicting the Tree of Jesse with carvings of saints and prophets; other houses retain overmantels showing Pentecost and the Judgement of Solomon. Outside the houses are decorated with carved wooden creatures – cherubs, lions and horses. In the house that is now the borough museum, the decoration was deemed to be so good that it was chosen as the place to entertain Charles II in 1671. A couple of years later, according to a lease, the buildings had begun to subside and so extra walls were built in the middle, running north to south, to support them. After this The Butterwalk seemed to remain untouched right up to the 1939-45 war when a German bomber swooped over the town and bombed it. Though The Butterwalk didn't suffer a direct hit, it was shaken and leaned over so badly that it was feared it might fall down.

After the war the plasterwork was carefully removed, piece by piece. At first it seemed as if the damage was irreparable. The council discussed pulling it down, but faced with the threat of losing the town's finest building, money was raised and it was restored with great care, putting back every piece of plaster. When local government was reorganised in 1974 and Dartmouth was merged into the greater unit of the South Hams, while all corporate property passed to Totnes, management of The Butterwalk and a few other buildings remained with the council at Dartmouth.

The Butterwalk, Dartmouth.

31

F. Young.

The Buckland Clock

Venture forth to Buckland-in-the-Moor and take a look at the church – or more specifically, the church clock. There are no numerals on the face, but in their place the words 'My Dear Mother'. There is no official explanation for this curiosity but one story tells of a local sailor boy. When news reached his mother that he had been lost at sea she refused to accept it, instead keeping a candle lit in her cottage window and food on the table in case her son should return. Amazingly the boy *did* return and so touched was he by his mother's faith that he put up the clock on the church tower in her memory when she died.

'My Dear Mother' replaces the more traditional figures on Buckland's clock.

Countess Weir – village of thatch?

A picture from photographer Ray Bishop, confirming the author's point about time moulding curiosity. Ray came to Countess Weir, near Exeter, in August 1953 – the summer of our Queen's Coronation – and immediately saw and understood why it was known as 'the village of thatch'. Yet when he went back to Countess Weir, a few years ago, all the thatched cottages had been demolished – and in their place were rows of bungalows!

Thatched cottages at Countess Weir.

Combe Martin and
some curious things

Isn't it curious how selective one's memory can be, the old adage of looking at the past with rose coloured glasses. As a small child I remember summers spent with my grandparents in Ilfracombe and the special treats at the end of the holiday such as a visit to the local ice-cream parlour for an enormous 'knickerbocker glory', or maybe a treat at home, a bowl of Combe Martin raspberries!

The village of Combe Martin lies in a fertile valley a few miles east of Ilfracombe and still produces large quantities of fruit and vegetables not only for Ilfracombe but for Lynton too. My grand-mother always reckoned that the finest raspberries in Britain came from Combe Martin and the potatoes too were always insisted upon. They just seemed to have more *taste*. I'm sure that the many visitors she entertained for bed, breakfast and evening meals over the years would agree – I know I do, or is that just nostalgia!

Combe Martin has several claims to fame.

It boasts the longest street of any village in England stretching one and three quarter miles from the London Inn to Nerwberry beach. It does actually change its name several times along the way – from Victoria Street to Castle Street, High Street, King Street, Seaside Street and finally to The Woodlands. I pity the poor postman who lands that route!

There are lost of odd looking houses all over Britain, indeed even Devon, but the Pack of Cards must rank as one of the most curious.

36

The Pack of Cards, Combe Martin.

In the eighteenth century George Ley won a large sum of money at a gaming table. To celebrate his success he built himself a house shaped like a pack of cards. There were originally 52 windows – one for each card in the pack – but some were bricked up when Prime Minister William Pitt introduced his window tax. No doubt Mr Ley did not want to part with more money to the Chancellor of the Exchequer than he had to. Some things don't change do they? There were four floors to represent the four suits, and, finally, each floor had 13 doors. The story goes that in the hallway stood a large oak table inside whose false top three men could hide from the Navy's Press Gang.

While people talk of the gold mines in Wales, and the Cornish tin mines, not many people know about the silver mines at Combe Martin. Apparently the rocks around the area are rich in galena ore, an important source of lead, and the silver present in them was supposed to be particularly rich. They were owned by the Crown from the time of Edward I and were known to have helped pay for the Hundred Years War in the reign of Edward III and Henry V.

The mines closed in 1480 but re-opened around 100 years later when a rich new lode was discovered. The biggest problem with the mines previously had been with the refining of the silver. However a gentleman called Bulmer, who originated from Somerset's Mendips found a way around the problem enabling a further six years of production. The most interesting relic of this episode is that there is still an object in existence made of Combe Martin silver mined from this period, some 400 years ago. It's a cup, one of two made by Bulmer. One was presented to the Marquess of Bath, the other to the Lord Mayor of London. The Lord Mayor's gift weighed in at a mighty 137 ounces – that's just over eight and a half pounds! – and was of superb quality. It's not surprising that in 1643 the cup was re-cast as 'lesser potts' and made into three tankards which are still at London's Mansion House where they are used at the Lord Mayor's annual banquet.

The original mining was opencast but gradually shafts were sunk and some say that parts of the actual village are undermined. Various attempts were made to re-open the mines until they were finally abandoned in 1875.

Exeter Airport

I have already stated that the definition of a curiosity is 'something unusual' which does not necessarily mean that it has to be hundreds of years old. Exeter Airport, which was officially opened in 1938, carved out from the land of Waterslade Farm, has its very own mystery dating from the 1939-45 war.

When the United States Army Air Force was preparing to leave Exeter after the war it had masses of unwanted aircraft and vehicle parts to get rid of. It has been suggested that the Americans simply bulldozed a huge crater in the centre of the grass triangle between the runways and buried all the debris. Another rumour suggests that there's another 'mechanical graveyard' somewhere else on the airfield, but no-one so far has put these rumours to the test. However, in these days of increased air travel the airport is expanding and the last thing they want is some enthusiast digging up the runways!

Exmouth and
Lady Nelson

It's a curious fact that we honour our glorious dead and pay homage to their memory but often the 'power behind the throne' – a wife or a husband – goes unremembered. Lord Nelson, one of Britain's greatest naval heroes, lies buried in St Paul's Cathedral, and his mistress Lady Hamilton ended up almost as famous as he. However, Lady Nelson, of which very little is generally known, was laid to rest at Exmouth, where she spent her last years.

Her house, now known locally as Nelson House is a Georgian red brick building on the Beacon which faces seaward. Frances Nisbet was a widow with a young son when she met Nelson, and while most historians would feel that they loved each other in their early years together, when Frances failed to bear him a son, Nelson developed what is euphemistically called 'a roving eye'.

Curiously, though the house is quite elegant-looking from the front, at the rear it's a real mish-mash of styles. The developer built the fronts to his houses and let the clients, who bought the houses, build the back. I wonder what our modern developers would make of that idea; I'm sure it would be a nightmare for the local planning department!

Anyway, Lady Nelson died here at the age of 73 and is buried in a corner of Littleham churchyard along with her son, Josiah and four of his children, all of whom died young. The tomb, a simpler copy of her

UNDERNEATH ARE DEPOSITED THE REMAINS OF

FRANCES HERBERT, VISCOUNTESS NELSON

DUCHESS OF BRONTI
WHO DEPARTED THIS LIFE
ON THE 6 OF MAY 1831 AGED 73 YEARS

ALSO HER SON JOSIAH NISBET
WHO DEPARTED THIS LIFE
ON THE 14 JULY 1830 AGED 50 YEARS
ALSO FOUR OF HIS CHILDREN
HORATIO WOOLWARD, HERBERT JOSIAH,
SARAH AND JOSIAH, ALL OF WHOM DIED YOUNG

Inscription on Lady Nelson's tomb.

husband's, has been restored and a new plaque has been placed on it.
Lady Nelson continues to rest, in the manner of her last years, with
dignity.

The red brick Nelson House at Exmouth.

Lady Nelson's tomb in Littleham Churchyard.

Finch Foundry
Sticklepath

In these days of protest against nuclear power, with some sections of the population advocating the use of alternative forms of energy, it seems we may go back to the days of the early industrialists and harness the power of the wind, the tides and the rivers.

In Devon, rivers were a vital factor in the life of many communities. A good example of this is Sticklepath, just outside Okehampton on the old road to Exeter.

The village was built on the River Taw which makes its way to Barnstaple. In fact the river is dammed about a half mile above the road bridge, and from there a leat travels down through Sticklepath to join the river again. Villagers constructed the leat to service Finch Foundry, built in 1814 under the leadership of William Finch, the village ironfounder. The business expanded taking over the corn and woollen mills and making cutting tools and shovels for the china clay workers, the farmers and the miners of Devon and Cornwall. Finch Foundry also made barrows and carts, gates and hurdles and even boat knees for the shipyards. For nearly 150 years the foundry flourished, providing employment for twenty men; at one stage there were even seven Finches working here.

But progress is a strange thing, sometimes it works for you, some-

Bob Barron who, with his sister, rescued the derelict foundry.

Finch Foundry Museum in 1983 when traffic roared through the village. Today the village is by-passed, enabling visitors to the foundry to call and leave easily in their cars. The by-pass has helped to bring sanity and safety back to Sticklepath.

times against. With the mass production of tools from the Midlands and the Northcountry and the greater use of machinery on the land, slowly the foundry's 'raison d'etre' died.

In 1960 when a wall collapsed it was an omen perhaps of the bankruptcy that was to follow. But, all was not lost. Richard Barron, a descendant of the Finch family decided to rescue it as a Museum of Rural Industry. Richard alas, died, but the project was taken on by Bob Barron and his sister Marjorie, and, aided by the goodwill of many, they achieved their goal.

Nowadays the machinery and water wheels – which once meant Sticklepath was called 'the village of water wheels' – survive and are regarded as 'the greatest possible value from an historical and educational point of view'. To visit the museum means a trip back in time. Watching the wheels sharpen a hook in the old-fashioned foundry way, it seems the power shears cut through iron as if it were butter. The Finch Foundry is no dull museum, it's a living personality, life injected back into it through the enthusiasm and love of Bob Barron and his sister and their band of helpers.

Mrs Rebecca Finch with her three sons and their families photographed in 1890.

Food Glorious Food

As a true Devonian I love my food. I have been known to enter deep discussions about the correct way to eat a Devonshire cream tea – should the jam be put on the scone first then followed by the cream or should it be the other way around? The answer lies in exactly where in Devon you were born! As a child I probably would never have consumed my mother's junket if it were not for the huge dollop of clotted cream on the surface which wobbled in unison with the junket in the dish. And I have excellent memories of devouring Grandma's treacle roly-poly topped with the very same thick yellow substance – yes, a dieter's nightmare. Here are a couple of stories about events held in Devon that concern food.

Branscombe is an attractive village on the south Devon coast between Sidmouth and Seaton and it used to hold an Apple Pie Fair each September.

Though no-one is quite sure how it all started it is thought that over 100 years ago some boys stole a very large apple pie from a local house, cut it up into neat slices and then sold it for pocket money. Not very honest, but certainly they showed a measure of enterprise. The local people obviously saw the funny side of it for they decided to celebrate the event by holding an annual Pie Fair, making huge apple pies some of which weighed up to half a hundredweight.

But if you think that's large then pause to consider the Paignton Pudding, a veritable culinary monster.

The original puddings were made as far back as the seventeenth century for the Paignton Fair, then drawn through the town and distributed afterwards.

In 1859 the railway came to Paignton, and to celebrate the event, the people elected a committee to organise the baking of a truly exceptional pud. Shaped like a pyramid, weighing in at one and a half tons and containing enormous quantities of flour, bread, fruit, eggs, sugar, suet, lemons, milk and spices it cost the princely sum of £45.

It was baked in eight sections then put together, and not content with a simple pudding for the feast, the committee provided 1900lbs of meat, 1900lbs of bread and plenty of cider to serve to the navvies who had built the railway, plus their wives and the poor of Paignton, Maridon and Stoke Gabriel. The great day came, August 1, with thousands of people coming to the town to watch the procession of the pudding with the navvies, picks and shovels in hand parading behind it. Paignton Green was the venue of the feast. Twelve large tables having been set up for the day, but just as their carvers began to slice, the crowd surged forward. The navvies, thinking that they would lose out, also charged into the throng and what should have been an orderly feast turned into a near riot!

Alarmed at the crowd the carvers began to throw slices of the pudding in all directions and the scramble only subsided when the last crumb of that splendid pudding was eaten. Incidentally, the Green is still *the* place in Paignton for any outdoor event be it a fair, a demonstration or a special occasion, like the William and Mary celebrations and the Royal visit in 1988.

Grimspound

'Time', so Erasmus once said, 'reveals all things'. Sometimes this proves case. High up on Dartmoor, north of Widecombe and just to the north of Hameldown Tor is Grimspound – all that time has left of an early Bronze Age village. The site itself covers some four acres with the remains of 24 hut circles – there are probably over 1,000 of these scattered on Dartmoor – and when I visited it, I could just imagine how our ancestors would have lived there, looking over the same exposed, sweeping landscape.

The huge slabs of granite were once attributed magical properties though the Moor at one time had a number of pagan religious structures of a similar kind to Stonehenge. Most were either demolished with the advent of Christianity and the stones used to build churches, or were simply removed by the local people to be used in more practical ways like farmhouse lintels, gateposts or bridges over the rivers. However, enough remains at Grimspound to show that it had particular religious significance.

The site was excavated in 1896 by Rev Sabine Baring-Gould, the squire and parson at Lewtrenchard who wrote many hymns – one of the best known being Onward Christian Soldiers – and Robert Burnard, a gifted amateur photographer. It was Burnard who first suggested that the solution to conserving Dartmoor's beauty was a national park and for many years he was Secretary of the Dartmoor Preservation Society. Baring-Gould was just as passionate about

Jane follows in the famous footsteps of the Rev Sabine Baring-Gould: a visit to Grimspound on a windswept morning in February.

conserving the Moor and he too was a founder member of the association.

Grimspound is worth visiting simply for its soul, its wild, stark beauty. Here you pinpoint earliest man's attempts to survive and where surely your own innate curiosity leads you to ponder, even for just a moment, what it must have been like to live at this spot, thousands of years ago.

Rev Sabine Baring-Gould steps up to Grimspound on a May morning in 1894.

Hot Cross Bun Memories

As a child, one of the nicest things about Easter-time was "the buns"
on Good Friday. As the day approached everyone would be asking,
'are you going down to the buns!' This custom of distributing buns
to the children of the town apparently is quite recent, dating from
around 1900.

The bakers of Sidmouth decided they were no longer going to
bake hot cross buns on Good Friday – rather a pity as my paternal
grandmother always claimed that a hot cross bun bought on Good
Friday would never go stale. She tried it one year but I never found
out if it remained edible; I think it was discreetly dispatched to the
dustbin after a while. So two enterprising Sidmouthians, a Mr Miller
and a Mr Goodwin went to Newton Poppleford, a village five miles
out of Sidmouth the other side of Four Elms Hill, and bought a large
supply of buns. They distributed them to children on the Bedford
Lawn, a large area – now a car park – beside the Bedford Hotel just a
few yards from the sea-front.

My father clearly remembers being taken to 'the buns' as a boy
and reckons the weather was usually good. There were few years I
can recall when the event had to be moved indoors because of bad
weather; somehow the sun would shine or at the very least it would
be cloudy with a bracing wind. My two nephews are now grown and
they are the third generation of my family to enjoy the custom, and we
are not an exception in the town. The event is remembered with such

affection that each new generation aupports it enthusiastically.

To me there was something fascinating about queuing around the car park, seeing the huge mounds of buns with the organisers standing at the ready. Mums and dads carrying babes in arms, brothers and sisters escorting the younger members of their families, and later, the coaches from the surrounding villages that brought in even more children. It was the anticipation of moving closer and closer to the tables; opening the paper bag and smelling the fresh baked buns. It was a time to meet with people that you never saw from one year to the next, people home for the Easter holiday. It was the walk across the sea front afterwards eating the spoils and ruining your appetite for lunch!

The Chairman of the Council – which when I was small was often my Uncle – always handed out the first bag. A photo was taken for the local paper, and Sidmouth Town Silver Band would lustily play from start to finish, long after the last bag had been handed out. I cannot remember there ever being a shortage, everyone had something, and by the time I walked around during the fifties and early sixties the two buns had an orange and a chocolate egg added to them. Long may this continue!

The House That Moved

You may well be assuming that some evil spirit or kindly pixie whisked this house in question away one night, but no, a modern curiosity based completely in fact!

Exeter, like many towns and cities, once suffered from a burgeoning traffic problem so the city fathers obviously had to produce a new road scheme. In the early sixties they encountered a problem; what to do with a house that some believed to be one of the oldest in Europe, dating from around 1430, and which stood slap bang in the way of the new scheme. Some people thought it should be demolished, others were determined it should be preserved at all costs, so a decision had to be made.

The conservationists won. On December 9 1961 the house was jacked up from its foundations, lifted onto a chassis with iron wheels and skilfully, but oh so gently, moved 100 yards along the road to its present site in West Street, safely tucked away from the pounding of the traffic. The journey took four days, but the house now stands, beautifully restored, as one of Exeter's great treasures.

Jolly Lane Cot

Back in 1835 it was still the custom on Dartmoor that if a house could be built with a roof in place between the hours of sunrise and sunset then the dwelling, and all the land enclosed around it, could be claimed by the builder. Still standing beside the stream at Huccaby, close to Hexworthy, is a small stone cottage. If you drove along the lane and passed by it you might just comment to a companion about this charming Dartmoor home, but in fact Jolly Lane Cot, as it is still known, has the distinction of being the last house in England to be built in a day.

The builders were Tom and Sally Satterly who chose Midsummer's Day to complete the task, probably because it was the day when most moorland folk would be attending the Ram Roasting Festival at Holne – an occasion now extinct. Their success in completing the house by the rules meant they were freed from their bonded employment and set up home as a free married couple.

Sally outlived Tom and became something of a Dartmoor legend before her death in 1901, sitting in her front doorway dressed in a black dress, white apron and white cap talking to passers by. She was fond of singing – the great Baring Gould once visited her to record her

The author visits Jolly Lane Cottage at Hucabby. This delightful cottage has become part of the folklore of Devon.

Our old picture postcard shows another face of Sally's cottage.

folk songs for posterity – and legend has it that she could shoe a horse, thatch a roof, cut a hay field or build a dry stone wall as well as any man. With such talents as these who *needs* a man around?

On her death the affection and respect she had earned was illustrated by the honour bestowed upon her by the Dartmoor people – a carrying funeral by the men of the moor across the tors and hills between Huccaby and Widecombe-in-the-Moor. On the way her coffin was rested on what is now the last 'coffin stone' left on Dartmoor, where the men would have changed over carrying teams, sung a hymn then completed the journey.

Passengers disembark from a launch on to a mobile landing stage which is hauled up Lundy's slipway by tractor.

The amazing tractor at Burgh Island.

An old postcard of Burgh Island with a tide swiftly covering the sand causeway that links the island to Bigbury-on-Sea.

Islands – Burgh
and Lundy

We are an island people. We can withdraw behind our shores and wait for the world to come to us, a sentiment perhaps that people who visit two curious islands off the Devon coast would agree with. Lundy Island in the north, is the larger of the two while Burgh Island lies in Bigbury Bay just three hundred yards from the mainland on the south coast.

Burgh Island is fascinating. It was originally called St Michael's after a chapel which stood on the top, like St Michael's Mount. Over the years the island was called La Burgh, the Burrow, until finally Burgh, and the chapel was replaced by a house and then a Huer's – or caller's – hut. A huer was a lookout for shoals of fish, so called because when fish were sighted a "hue and cry" was made to alert the fishermen waiting on the shore. The fish in question were pilchards. Each July and August the shoals set off from west of the Scilly Isles and hugged the coast as far as Bigbury Bay. When caught, they were usually stored in buildings on the island until the oil was extracted and exported to the Mediterranean.

Sadly the pilchard industry here is no more, all that's left is the inn on the island named after the fish who provided the livelihood for so many people in the area. It dates back to the fourteenth century and was once a haunt for local pirates: it is even said that one of them, Tom Crocker still haunts the inn.

To reach the island there's a unique mode of transport, a sea tractor. Though the island is just a short distance from the mainland

and can be reached on foot at low tide, the currents are particularly tricky for boats to make the crossing and so the tractor was devised. The vehicle was made by a firm in Newton Abbot, Beares, and was specially designed to cope with the crossing. It can carry up to 40 people, can operate in up to seven feet of water and moves at four miles per hour.

Apart from the inn on the island there is an hotel, recently refurbished by the island's owners. It was built in 1929 by Archibald Nettlefold who created a luxury retreat for the wealthy who desired to 'get away from it all'. Noel Coward and Agatha Christie were just two well known visitors. The hotel also has a sea pool and Nettlefold had all the gaps filled in to retain the sea water when the tide fell. In the centre was a platform so in the 1930s a visitor might stroll outside to look and listen to the band which had rowed across and, under floodlights, played the night away.

Lundy Island, off Devon's northern coast, is mugh bigger and wild, though it, too, has its share of pirates and tractors! Indeed, the landing stage that is used when visitors make the trip across from Ilfracombe is drawn down into the sea by a tractor, though landings – or leave-takings – will not be made when the wind blows from the east. As for pirates, not much is known of the history of the island before the twelfth century when the island was owned by the Marisco family. They became pirates and took to harassing the neighbours, while much later, in the early seventeenth century, pirates were fairly commonplace it seems and, as Lundy was the haunt of these rogues, the island was often attacked by the Spanish and the French. No doubt they were trying to retrieve stolen property!

The name Lundy derives from the Scandinavian 'lundi' which means puffin and these birds still nest on the island in large numbers. The ownership of the island has changed hands several times though one interesting owner in the nineteenth century was W H Heaven. He proclaimed Lundy to be a 'free island' and successfully resisted the attempts of jurisdiction from the mainland. Lundy was some-times colloquially known as the 'kingdom of Heaven'!

The island is three miles long, half a mile wide and lies north to south in the Bristol channel. As a child I remember thinking it was always a mysterious far away place, to be viewed on a fine day from the mainland, and one that I might never visit. Nowadays it is owned by the National Trust which ensures that the flora, fauna and wildlife, for which Lundy is famous, remains intact. The few buildings that

The steep cliffs of Lundy drop dramatically into the Bristol Channel.

stand are also protected: the two lighthouses, one at each end of the island, the church of St Helen, and, at the south east corner, the keep of the old Marisco castle, now converted into cottages. Like Burgh Island, there is a pub and a hotel to visit, and, while the last adjective you would use to describe Lundy is glamorous, it can boast a literary

St Helen's Church, Lundy.

connection inasmuch that Charles Kingsley described in Westward Ho! how Don Guzman's ship was wrecked off of Shutter Rock.

Finally the granite from Lundy was used, not only for many parish churches in Devon, but was taken up to London too. Next time you stroll along the Thames embankment, cast your eyes up and down. You'll be looking at Lundy granite and I leave Lundy with this

The mysterious, dark Quarry Pool.

charming little verse that is probably as accurate a weather forecast I have ever come across: 'Lundy high, sure to be dry; Lundy low, bound to be snow; Lundy plain, going to be rain; Lundy haze, fine for days'.

The Nobody Inn
Doddiscombsleigh

How often do you use a name without thinking of its origins, particularly when it comes to pubs? We probably all do it quite often without a second thought. But names are curious. Often they just 'stick' for no reason at all while others have more traditional origins. There's an inn between Newton Abbot and Exeter at Doddiscombsleigh, a village which nestles in a combe under the western slopes of Haldon in the Teign valley. It is called The Nobody Inn, and there are several 'tales' about the origin of the name.

The name is quite recent for up to 1937 it was known as The New Inn. One story suggests that the landlord at this time died in an Exeter hospital, but at his funeral, an empty coffin was buried. The undertakers and bearers thought the coffin was light, but then reasoned that, after all, the landlord had been ill for some time. As recently as 1970 a retired police superintendent visited the pub from Norfolk and he said the story was quite true for he had been a probationary constable at the Exeter coroner's office in the late 1930s and he remembered an exhumation order being granted to allow the grave to be opened.

Another story tells of a retired major, who was quite wealthy, and did not really need customers. He did like the inn though, and closed the doors, opening them only to his friends. Meanwhile a third story relates to the landlord and landlady going out on market day and leaving the pub door open with a note on the counter requesting

Sixteenth century The Nobody Inn, Doddiscombsleigh, near Exeter.

patrons to help themselves because there was 'nobody in'. Oh yes, and could they please put the money in the tin provided.

Finally, it is said that an unknown landlord refused hospitality to weary travellers who passed by. When no-one replied to the knocking they continued their journey believing there was 'nobody in' and 'Nobody Inn' it has remained ever since.

No matter how the name came about the inn remains charming. The buildings and pub are definitely much older than the name, based on late fifteenth - early sixteenth century terraced cottages, a sort of 'one up - two down' design, the end one being a cider house, a traditional feature in this type of village. Additions were made by converting old stables or outhouses so that today the inn looks like a large rambling cottage, surrounded by a pretty cottage garden. You can still stay at the inn if you wish, but it is extremely popular for its food and drink. The cellar boasts traditionally brewed beer, over 120 whiskies and more than 400 wines, ports and home-made mulled wine. There is also a vast range of locally produced foods particularly cheese.

Incidentally, if you visit the inn, try and spare a moment to look into the fifteenth century church of St Michael. There are five large windows in the aisle and apart from four windows in Exeter cathedral, these at Doddiscombsleigh church are the only complete windows of medieval glass left in Devon.

The Flaming Tar
Barrels of
Ottery St Mary

Ottery St Mary in East Devon is a town which holds very pleasant memories for me. For seven years I travelled the six or so miles from Sidmouth by bus to attend King Henry VIII Grammar School. I have clear pictures of attending services at the Church of St Mary every term, almost freezing to death on the exposed pitches during the hockey season, and attending one of the most exciting customs in East Devon, the 'flaming tar barrels'.

Every year on November 5 Ottery holds its carnival, the procession taking place in the evening. A huge bonfire is built in a meadow just by the river with a Guy Fawkes effigy tied to the top. The custom of lighting large fires at this time of year goes back beyond the days of the gunpowder plot though. A large bonfire was lit at the end of the harvest indicating the beginning of winter. In Ottery, once the carnival is over and the bonfire lit it is the turn of the tar barrels.

Each hotel or pub gives its name to a barrel and some weeks before the event the barrels are soaked with tar. On the great day, the barrels are brought forth, ignited and gently rolled around until the whole of the inside is alight. Quickly, one of the men taking part will hoist the barrel aloft, place it on his shoulders and run as fast as he can down the main street scattering screaming spectators from his path, protecting himself by wearing thick gloves made of sacking. When he can hold the barrel no longer it is taken up by another man

who again runs with it, and so the process goes on until the barrel disintegrates and is left to die out quietly where it has fallen.

The men then move on to the next pub – there's usually about eight in all – and start all over again. You have to be pretty fit, not to mention brave to take part, as you could be running around until midnight. In the afternoon there is a 'boy's barrel' on a smaller but no less enthusiastic scale and I must make mention of the 'lady's barrel' in the evening which definitely adds to the thrills of the evening, and woe betide any man who tries to interfere!

Over the years various attempts have been made to stop the barrels but such is the support from the local community, not to mention the crowds who come to support the event from all over East Devon, the custom still remains.

Curious though it may seem, Ottery is not the only place in which this strange custom takes place, for in the market town of Hatherleigh, on the very same night a similar scene may be encountered.

The Fire Festival at Ottery St Mary: '... blazing tar barrels are carried through the streets.'

Plymouth Curiosities
Derry's Clock
and Citadel Gate

The bombing raids of the 1939-45 war were responsible for demolishing large parts of the towns and cities of Britain and the Westcountry was not exempt, the city of Plymouth being the worst hit in Devon. This fine city which, up to 1914 was known as the three towns because it grew from Stonehouse, Devonport and Plymouth. It had flourished in and survived many wars from as far back as the sixteenth century, but it was pounded from the air between 1940 and 1943, suffering vast damage and casualties.

A new city has, of course, risen proudly from the ruins but it's a curious thing to see what architectural monuments to Plymouth's past glory remain. Indeed, it has not only been a question of surviving a war, the developers have also moved in and demolished buildings that some people would have preferred left standing.

Derry's Clock survives from 1863 when it was built by Plymouth Corporation. Most of the money was given by William Derry the then mayor who was a Liberal, and the son of a Sherwell deacon. He was a director of the Plymouth Tramways Company formed under the Act of 1870 which held the contract for all the local horse transport for the Great Western. He was typical of the mayors of the time being a man of substance, a professional man and a leader of the community in the fullest sense.

At the eastern end of the Hoe you will still find the Citadel, one of

The Citadel, Plymouth captured on an old photograph.

Derry's Clock, Plymouth.

the most important historic buildings left in Plymouth. Though there had been earlier defensive buildings at Plymouth the fort still standing dates from 1666, and the foundation stone laid by John Grenville, then Governor, can still be seen. The Citadel Gate actually dates from 1670, the work of Sir Thomas Fitz – though often attributed to Sir Christopher Wren. It's one of the best examples of baroque architecture in the country and quite unlike anything else in the West of England.

Plymouth suffered badly from German bombing in the last war. This photograph of soldiers and sailors digging among the ruins is a vivid reminder of the horror of the Plymouth blitz. Incredibly Jane's two choices for Plymouth curiosities both survived that terrible hammering from the sky.

Sidmouth –
a right royal
place to sleep

There are several items in this book that have sparked off a childhood recollection for me – and this is one. The Royal Glen Hotel, tucked just back from Sidmouth's sea front was a building pointed out to me from an early age, usually when I was being cajoled by my parents to 'keep up and cheer up' on a family walk. 'Queen Victoria stayed there' I was told. It didn't really mean very much then, and I promptly forgot all about it. Now, being much older and wiser, I view this building in a totally different light. I'm rather proud of this royal connection and am pleased to be able to explain how it came about.

At the turn of the nineteenth century the Napoleonic wars prevented the middle-class tourist from visiting continental resorts so an alternative was sought. Though not having the glorious sunshine of the French Riviera, Sidmouth could at least boast a milder climate than many other parts of the country, so it became a fashionable watering hole. In 1819 it was given a definite fillip by the arrival of royalty. The Duke of York, fourth son of King George III, decided, like many other people then, to build a home by the sea – and I thought that second homes were a twentieth century invention! A 'cottage by the sea' sounds quite modest to you or me, but the Duke's ideas were somewhat different. He built Woolbrook Cottage, later to be renamed The Royal Glen. The house more accurately resembles a medieval house with its Gothic pointed windows and a verandah complete with roof terrace and french doors. Originally

Woolbrook Cottage – The Duke of York's quiet little place by the sea at Sidmouth was a bit grand for the title 'cottage'.

given the gauche label of 'cottage orne' – in English simply ornate cottage – it later was simply known as Regency.

The interior followed suit with elaborate designs and comfortable furnishings. The drawing rooms boast a fireplace designed and carved by Robert Adam and the Duke and Duchess's bedrooms bave been altered very little.

The Duke arrived with his wife, who suffered from poor health and thus welcomed a milder climate, and his baby daughter Victoria, later to be Queen. He liked Sidmouth. He was, after all, out of sight of his mad father and elder brother William, then Prince Regent. But most important, he was away from his creditors who couldn't trace him to Sidmouth from his mail as it was posted to Salisbury in Wiltshire. Regular trips were made there to collect it. He would push Victoria up and down the sea front, perhaps pausing to speak to a passer-by to show off his beautiful child like any proud parent.

Curiously, this tiny child, who was to become such a formidable Queen, had a lucky escape from death when a young boy, shooting at sparrows outside missed his prey and his shot smashed one of the panes in the window of the nursery where the young princess lay sleeping. Imagine how history would have been changed if Victoria had been hit and had died. The pane was replaced by a piece of coloured glass which is still there.

It was on one of his regular trips to Salisbury to collect his post that the Duke caught a chill and soon after died, which was sad for he was soon to become heir to the throne. However, his death left the route clear for Victoria, though at the time she did not know where her duties would lie. When told that she would one day be queen she simply replied 'I shall be good'.

The Spanish Barn
Torre Abbey

The site of Torre Abbey is one of the oldest in Torquay, thought to have been held by Alric at the Norman Conquest, but passed on from hand to hand until at the time of the Crusades, it was owned by the De Briwer family. A member of that family was held hostage during the Crusade of Richard I and in return for his release the Pope and the Premonstratensian Order of Canons were promised some land on which to build an Abbey. Twelve months later, in 1196, the first abbot arrived with his canons, dressed in their traditional white habits to found the 23rd such house in England at that time.

The tithe barn that stands beside the abbey is commonly known as the 'Spanish Barn'. By the time of the Armada the abbey had been 'dissolved' by Henry VIII in 1539 and had eventually passed to Sir Edward Seymour of Berry Pomeroy. Some of the Armada was fought in Torbay and in the June of 1588 one of the ships, the Nuestra Senora del Rosario, was captured by Drake and brought ashore at Torre Abbey.

The Nuestra was the 'Capitana' or flag ship of the Andalusian squadron and while her commander, Don Pedro de Valdez and his officers were taken aboard Drake's own ship Revenge, the crew were locked up in the tithe barn, all 397 of them. Here they were to remain until August 18 when they were divided into three groups and taken away, some to the town prison at Exeter, some to the Bridewell and the rest to Dartmouth. The cost of maintaining the prisoners was

fourpence a day, borne totally by Sir George Cary of Cockington, a branch of whose family was later to own the abbey and barn itself.

Nowadays the barn has been much restored to its original appearance, by Torquay Corporation who bought it in 1930; the only remaining piece of the original roof is preserved in the abbey and in the course of digging up the floor a cannon ball was found, one of many discovered in the area. In the centre of the barn's floor lies the following inscription:

The Spanish Barn built 1196
Herein 397 prisoners of war from the Spanish
galleon Nuestra Senora del Rosario
were incarcerated, July 26th, 1588.

The Spanish Barn boasts a ghost. Peter Underwood, President of The Ghost Club, on his tour of haunted Devon for Bossiney's bestselling 'Ghosts of Devon' recalled the phantom form of a young Spanish girl 'seen drifting sadly through the park . . .'

Stories about stone

No journey among the curiosities of Devon would be complete without some reference to its ancient stones. There are thousands of prehistoric monuments in Devon, of one sort or another, most of which are on Dartmoor, but here are just a few stories about stones scattered at other parts of the county.

Firstly to the north. Just outside of Morte Point at Mortehoe there is the Morte Stone, many ships have been wrecked on it, and legend has it that it can be removed by a husband who can and will assert that he, and not his wife, is the master in the house. Another version says that a consortium of wives could have the same effect. Any others?

Further along the coast at Appledore there's a flat stone called the Wibblestone. The story goes that Appledore was the place reached by Hubba The Dane when he left the Welsh Coast . . . 'to waste with fire and sword . . .' according to those around in King Alfred's day, and expected to maintain his success rate in North Devon. Not so, he underestimated Devon's ancestors who slayed all of Hubba's men, with Hubba himself being buried on the shore covered by stones as was the Scandinavian tradition. Of course the stones were soon washed away, but it is said that Hubba was buried beneath this flat stone, the Wibblestone, and the spot became known as Bloody Corner. The spot was apparently haunted and passers-by removed

Spinsters Rock at Shilstone. Legend says that three spinsters put it up one morning but it seems more likely some Bronze Age chaps did the lifting a little earlier in history.

their shoes and stockings in case they should be heard and rouse the ghost.

Then to the east of the county, between Honiton and Sidmouth, the Hunters Lodge stone, also known as Putts Corner stone, thought to be a slaughter stone for a particular band of witches and which has the ability, along with a neighbouring stone to get up and go places. If it hears the clock strike twelve it tracks down the valley for a drink or some say to wash off the blood in the River Sid while the stone

Many ships have been wrecked on the Morte Stone, off Morte Point.

nearby merely turns round three times when it hears midnight strike.

Finally to the edge of Dartmoor, Drewsteignton, or specifically to Shilstone and Spinsters Rock. It is probably the remains of a Bronze Age megalithic tomb but legend has it that three unmarried ladies erected it one morning and it is the only cromlech – an ancient structure of large stones set on end supporting a stone laid horizontally – left in Devon.

A miniature Versailles in Paignton

Nowadays Isaac Singer would be dubbed 'nouveau riche' if the fortune he amassed with his sewing machines were made today. However, money is money, and what Mr Singer did with some of his was to build a magnificent home at Paignton. Isaac Singer was of humble birth. His father had emigrated to America from Germany and Isaac's unique sewing machines were the first to have needles threaded at the pointed end, enabling the thickest of cloths to be sewn.

In 1871 Isaac bought the Fernham estate at Paignton and began to build his home. It was completed by 1874 and originally called 'The Wigwam'. It was magnificent. Costing more than £100,000 it was designed by G S Bridgeman, but Isaac's son Paris obviously wasn't happy with the finished house, for when he took it over he remodelled Oldway almost completely, and by 1904 only the western elevation remained untouched.

Paris decided to make it into a miniature Versailles and set about altering three of the elevations to resemble Louis XIV's great palace. Inside he put in a grand marble staircase, an exact replica of the one in France, which divided at a central landing and matched each piece of marble at each joint. The vaulted ceiling, supported on huge columns, again is an exact replica from the French palace and so insistent was Paris that detail should be correctly reproduced that he arranged for scaffolding to be erected at Versailles so that his painter could study the painting of the original artist, Lebrun.

Another stunning feature of the interior was the ballroom, with

The magnificent home built by the Singer family of sewing machine fame. Father Isaac spent over £100,000 on the new house at Ferndown estate, Paignton, but when his son Paris inherited it he almost completely remodelled the mansion.

its sprung floor, chandeliers and minstrels gallery, based on the famous Hall of Mirrors. Paris, like his father before him, dallied outside of his marriage. His relationship with the dancer Isadora Duncan is well known and it was for her that the ballroom was designed. However, Paris' mother Isabella was not without beauty for she became the model for one of the most famous pieces of sculpture in the world, the Statue of Liberty.

His fascination with French art extended to paintings and in 1898 Paris purchased a painting by Jacques David of Napoleon at his coronation crowning Josephine. The canvas, measuring 18 feet by 30 feet, was bought for 32,000 francs but in 1946 it was sold back to the French Government and now hangs – in Versailles!

The family ceased to live in the house in 1914 and for a few years the house was put to various uses until finally it was bought by the local authority in 1946 for £45,000. Finally, if you visit this splendid property, which is the venue for many marriages each week of the year, note the Rotunda just opposite the entrance. If you think that also has a familiar look to it, let me tell you that it is a miniature version of the Albert Hall, originally designed to be used here as a riding pavilion. Now that is what I call riding out in style!

Widecombe

Of all the local folk songs that have originated in Devon I would happily stick my neck out and say that the best known would be Widecombe Fair, telling the sad tale of Uncle Tom Cobley and his merry band.

It is probably this song, first published in 1880, that has made Widecombe the popular tourist attraction of today though once you visit it you will soon find out several interesting facts about this Dartmoor village which covers 11,000 acres of Dartmoor making it the second largest in the county of Devon.

Without doubt the most famous thing to come out of Widecombe is Uncle Tom. Interestingly, one Thomas Cobley was born, not in Widecombe but in the village of Spreyton in 1762, and died there in 1844. His grave can still be seen in the churchyard and he probably collected his motley crew for Widecombe in the sixteenth century pub, then called the White Hart but now named after their most famous son. The fair that Uncle Tom rode to is still held on the second Tuesday in September and is a hive of activity with sheep and ponies. The current Uncle Tom is Peter Hicks, a hill farmer who has lived in the village at Higher Venton for the past 40 years. Each year he dons the traditional costume for the fair and enters into the spirit of the proceedings with great relish.

The village of Widecombe nestles in the East Webburn valley, surrounded by ridges and tors with scattered dwellings made of rough hewn granite and often topped with thatch. These days

The author visits Beatrice Chase's grave at Widecombe churchyard –
Olive Katharine Parr being the real name of that great Dartmoor
eccentric and author: a woman who became a legend in her curious
lifetime.

though, as Peter Hicks explained to me, the cost of repairing a thatch can sometimes, sadly, prove prohibitive. Peter's own house dates back to 1560 and along with most of the farm buildings is listed as being of historical importance. The original house was extended over the years, particularly by its most famous occupant, Beatrice Chase, who bought the property in 1904 when she moved to Dartmoor with her mother.

Beatrice, whose real name was Olive Katharine Parr, was born in Harrow, Middlesex in 1874 and was a rather eccentric, enigmatic character. She claimed to be a direct descendant of Catherine Parr – the sixth wife of Henry VIII – once thought of entering the Dominican Order, she visited Dartmoor Prison working for reform in the prison system and, during the 1914-18 war, began a crusade asking all men to lead clean lives!

However, she is most famous for books on Dartmoor. A tall, handsome woman, her writing earned her a loyal following and much respect among the local community. Her best books were *Through A Dartmoor Window* and *The Heart Of The Moor*. A woman of redoubtable energy and drive she also became a professional photographer – her book of *Dartmoor Snapshots*, published in 1931 is now a collector's item – and bookseller, selling autographed copies of her books and picture postcards at Venton House.

Sadly the rollercoaster of success came to an end for her around 1940. Beatrice became a recluse relying on the telephone for her contact with the outside world. It is said she sometimes made up to 90 calls a day on what she called: 'my blimming telephone'. She will be remembered, not only for her books and photographs but, for her passion in defending the moor from progress; incidentally, she carried on a vigorous opposition to the establishment of the moor as a national park. Beatrice left quite specific instructions in her will that she should be buried at Venton at the top of a field near the house. Instead she lies, peacefully I hope, in a quiet corner of the church of St Pancras in the village. I'm sure she would be pleased to know that as we speed towards the end of the twentieth century there are still many people who care as much about retaining the moor's natural beauty as she did.

The two faces of Peter Hicks – talking to Jane in his role as hill farmer and, as Uncle Tom Cobley, at Widecombe Fair.

If you have ever visited Widecombe you may well understand this question and its answer correctly:

"When is an Inn not an Inn?"

Answer: "when it's a cottage".

Yes, an inn that looks to all intents and purposes like a cottage. The Rugglestone Inn at Widecombe, built as a cottage, became an inn in 1850 the first licensee being farmer and stonemason, James Lee.

By 1923 the Lamb family had taken over and the inn is still run by one of their descendants. It is situated just a half mile walk from the church and while the exterior may be deceptive to the passer-by, the interior would certainly surprise any prospective customer.

There is no bar, the beer being served from a narrow taproom which opens onto the passage and you drink in what is effectively the front parlour. Though the inn was connected to mains electricity in the 1960s the proprietors have retained one calor gas lamp – just for an emergency. The beauty and unique nature of the Rugglestone lies in its delightful character, virtually untouched by the passage of time. No mock fittings or restoration, this is all original and long may it remain so.

Wife Sales

Writing now in the latter part of the twentieth century with high divorce figures almost taken for granted, it is curious to find that some of our ancestors had their own way of dealing with a marriage that seemed, in today's parlance, to have 'irretrievably broken down'. It was deemed to be right and proper in some men's eyes to sell their wives when things didn't work out, one man leading his wife into Okehampton market where she was bought by a local poet for half a crown. He then led his new 'wife' home by a halter which she placidly wore in a loop around her neck.

The woman proved an excellent wife being thrifty, clean, tactful and respectful, but when she died, around 1843, there was a problem with the local parson about under which name she should be buried. Eventually, after much argument as to her legal name the man carried her off to the next parish where they obviously didn't mind what her name was!

Another Plymouth man, a publican, paid for his wife with a two gallon jar of Plymouth gin. She had previously belonged to a stonecutter who put up the following notice in several public places:

This here be to inform the publick as how James Cole be dispozed to sell his wife by Auction. Her be a decent, clanely woman, and be of age twenty-five years. The sale be to take place in the New Inn, Thursday next at seven o'clock.

On the day of the sale the woman was made to stand on a table.

Mr Cole armed himself with a small hammer and informed the assembled throng that biddings were to be in kind and not in money, for he believed the sale would be illegal if money passed hands. One man offered a coat, but as he was a small man and the seller was stout he refused; another man offer a "phisgie", a pick, but that was no use as Mr Cole already owned one. Finally the landlord offered the gin and the hammer came down with 'Gone'!

There are other tales of wife sales at North Bovey and Chagford and at Great Torrington, where a man put a reserve price on his wife, of just eighteen pence. Unfortunately no-one would give so much money so he had to take his wife home again and take up where they had left off.

Westward Ho!

Now here's a strange thing, a town developed on the success of a book. Westward Ho, just outside of Northam in North Devon was built by a company formed after the publication of Charles Kingsley's book of the same name in 1855. First, the Westward Ho Hotel was built, then a church – in 1870 – a couple of years later a few rows of houses and a golf course, known as one of the best in England. In 1874 the United Services College for the sons of officers was opened and was used by another writer, Rudyard Kipling for the setting of Stalky & Co.

Alas, in time, less thought was given to planning and nowadays, while the golf course remains superb, the most interesting item to look at is the Pebble Ridge, a remarkable natural phenomenon nearly two miles long, 50 feet wide and 20 feet high.

Charles Kingsley's statue at Bideford.

Also Available

DARTMOOR IN THE OLD DAYS
James Mildren

DART — THE MAGICAL RIVER
Ken Duxbury

GHOSTS OF DEVON
Peter Underwood

HISTORIC INNS OF DEVON
Monica Wyatt

MYSTERIES IN THE DEVON LANDSCAPE
Hilary Wreford & Michael Williams

HIDDEN KNOWLEDGE
Lori Reid

CASTLES OF DEVON
James Mildren

UNKNOWN DEVON
Rosemary Anne Lauder, Michael Williams & Monica Wyatt

LEGENDS OF DEVON
Sally Jones

STRANGE STORIES FROM DEVON
Rosemary Anne Lauder & Michael Williams

PLYMOUTH IN WAR & PEACE
Guy Fleming

PEOPLE & PLACES IN DEVON
Monica Wyatt

DARTMOOR PRISON
Rufus Endle

SUPERNATURAL ADVENTURE
Michael Williams

We shall be pleased to send you our catalogue giving full details of our growing list of titles for Devon, Cornwall, Dorset, Somerset and Wiltshire as well as forthcoming publications. If you have difficulty in obtaining our titles, write direct to Bossiney Books, Land's End, St Teath, Bodmin, Cornwall.